A Little Green Dandelion

by Jane Scoggins Bauld
illustrated by Cathy Morrison

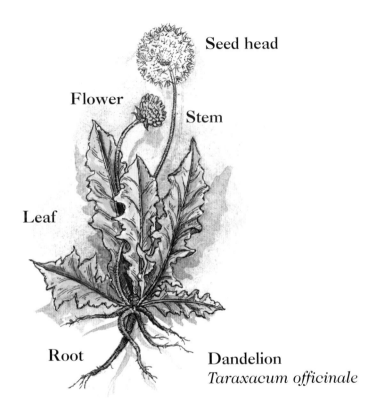

Seed head

Flower

Stem

Leaf

Root

Dandelion
Taraxacum officinale

 **Richard C. Owen Publishers, Inc.**
Katonah, New York

A little green dandelion grew
up through a crack in a gritty,
city sidewalk.

The sun helped it grow.

The rain helped it grow.

It grew bigger, and bigger,
and bigger.

3

A boy rode his bicycle over it.

A cat sat on it while she washed
her face and ears with her paw.

A mail carrier stepped on it
with his big, heavy shoe.

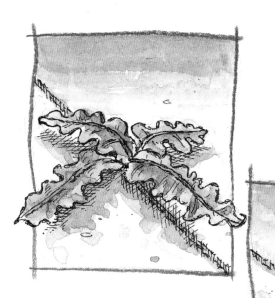

The little green dandelion
got smaller,

and smaller,

and smaller.

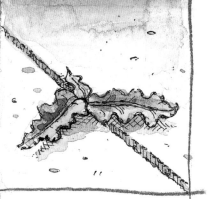

Soon, only a few crumpled
leaves were left.

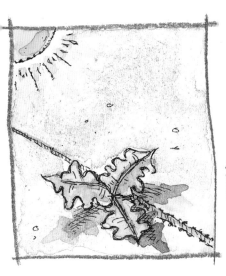

The little green dandelion's roots were deep and strong, and it began to grow again.

The sun helped it grow.

The rain helped it grow.

It grew bigger, and bigger, and bigger.

One day the little green dandelion grew a bright, yellow flower.

After a while, the flower became
a ball of soft, white fuzz.

A little girl walked down the street
and picked the little dandelion.
She blew on it, and its white fuzz flew all about,
then slowly drifted to the ground.

Soon, lots of little green dandelions
grew up through cracks in the city's gritty sidewalk.
The sun helped them grow.
The rain helped them grow . . .